First World War
and Army of Occupation
War Diary
France, Belgium and Germany

1 DIVISION
Divisional Troops
Royal Army Medical Corps
3 Field Ambulance
5 August 1914 - 31 July 1915

WO95/1259/1

The Naval & Military Press Ltd
www.nmarchive.com
Published in association with The National Archives

Published by

The Naval & Military Press Ltd

Unit 10 Ridgewood Industrial Park,

Uckfield, East Sussex,

TN22 5QE England

Tel: +44 (0) 1825 749494

www.naval-military-press.com

www.nmarchive.com

This diary has been reprinted in facsimile from the original. Any imperfections are inevitably reproduced and the quality may fall short of modern type and cartographic standards.

© Crown Copyright
Images reproduced by permission of The National Archives, London, England, 2015.

Contents

Document type	Place/Title	Date From	Date To
Heading	WO95/1259/1 3 Field Ambulance Aug 14-July 15		
Heading	B.E.F. France & Flanders 1 Division Troops. 3 Field Ambulance. 1914 Aug To 1915 July (To Guards Division) 141 Field Ambulance. 1916 July To 1919 June 13 Sanitary Section. 1915 Apr To 1917 Mar. 2 Mobile Veterinary Section. 1914 Aug To 1919 Aug.		
Heading	1st Division Medical 3rd Field Ambulance 1914 Aug-1915 July To Guards Div		
Heading	War Diary No 3 Field Ambulance (1st Infantry Divn) Volume I		
War Diary	Aldershot	05/08/1914	18/08/1914
War Diary	Southampton	18/08/1914	18/08/1914
War Diary	Boulogne	19/08/1914	21/08/1914
War Diary	Aulnoye	22/08/1914	22/08/1914
War Diary	Beaufort	22/08/1914	22/08/1914
War Diary	Grand Reng	23/08/1914	27/08/1914
War Diary	Etrieux	27/08/1914	27/08/1914
War Diary	Bernot	27/08/1914	28/08/1914
War Diary	Bertancourt	28/08/1914	29/08/1914
War Diary	Vaux Boin Pres Soissons	30/08/1914	31/08/1914
War Diary	Missy Le Bois	31/08/1914	31/08/1914
Heading	121/1078 War Diary No 3 Field Ambulance Volume II		
War Diary	Coulommiers	03/09/1914	03/09/1914
War Diary	Mourock	04/09/1914	04/09/1914
War Diary	Rozoy	05/09/1914	05/09/1914
War Diary	Pompierre	06/09/1914	06/09/1914
War Diary	Vaddoy	07/09/1914	07/09/1914
War Diary	Dagny	08/09/1914	08/09/1914
War Diary	Sablonnierre	09/09/1914	09/09/1914
War Diary	Priez	11/09/1914	11/09/1914
War Diary	Lhuys	12/09/1914	12/09/1914
War Diary	Bourg	13/09/1914	14/09/1914
War Diary	Vendresse	15/09/1914	18/09/1914
War Diary	Villers	19/09/1914	30/09/1914
Heading	121/1818 Oct-1914 S No 3 Field Ambulance Vol III		
War Diary	Villers	08/10/1914	31/10/1914
Heading	121/2671 Nov. 1914 S No 3 Field Ambulance Vol IV		
War Diary		01/11/1914	09/11/1914
War Diary	Ypres	16/11/1914	16/11/1914
War Diary	Locre	17/11/1914	17/11/1914
War Diary	Oultersteen	18/11/1914	28/11/1914
Heading	No 3 Field Ambulance Vol V		
War Diary		01/12/1914	03/12/1914
War Diary	Outtersteen	03/12/1914	31/12/1914
War Diary	Bethune	31/12/1914	31/12/1914
Heading	121/4257 jan 1915. No 3 Field Ambulance Vol VI		
War Diary	Bathune	01/01/1915	16/01/1915
War Diary	Beuvry	16/01/1915	27/01/1915
War Diary	Bethune	28/01/1915	31/01/1915
Heading	121/4657 Oct 1915 3rd Field Ambulance Vol VII		

War Diary	Bethune	01/02/1915	03/02/1915
War Diary	La Beuvriere	04/02/1915	27/02/1915
War Diary	Bethune	28/02/1915	28/02/1915
Heading	121/4807 March 1915 S No 3 Field Ambulance Vol VIII		
War Diary	Bethune	01/03/1915	31/03/1915
Heading	121/5161 April 1915 No 3 Field Ambulance Vol IX		
War Diary	Bethune	01/04/1915	30/04/1915
Heading	July 1915 121/5513 No 3 Field Ambulance Vol X		
War Diary	Bethune	01/05/1915	22/05/1915
War Diary	Fouquieres	25/05/1915	31/05/1915
Heading	121/6210 June 1915 1st Division No 3 Field Ambulance Vol XI		
War Diary	Fouquieres	01/06/1915	20/06/1915
Heading	121/6210 July 1915 1Division No 3 Field Ambulance Vol XII		
War Diary	Fouquieres	01/07/1915	31/07/1915

WO95/1259 ①

3 Field Ambulance
Aug '14 – July '15

B.E.F. FRANCE & FLANDERS
1 DIVISION. TROOPS.

3 FIELD AMBULANCE.
1914 AUG TO 1915 JULY
(TO GUARDS DIVISION)

141 FIELD AMBULANCE.
1916 JULY TO 1919 JUNE

13 SANITARY SECTION.
1915 APR TO 1917 MAR.

2 MOBILE VETERINARY SECTION.
1914 AUG TO 1919 AUG.

1259

B.E.F. FRANCE & FLANDERS.
1 DIVISION.   TROOPS.
3 FIELD AMBULANCE.
1914 AUG TO 1915 JULY.
(TO GUARDS DIVISION)
141 FIELD AMBULANCE.
1916 JULY TO 1919 JUNE.
13 SANITARY SECTION.
1915 APR TO 1917 MAR.
2 MOBILE VETERINARY
            SECTION.
1914 AUG TO 1919 AUG.

1st Division

Medical

3rd Field Ambulance

~~January to July 1915~~

1914 AUG — 1915 JULY

TO GUARDS DIV

12/5/12
Aug. 1914

WAR DIARY

No 3. Field Ambulance (1st September Divⁿ)

Volume I.

WAR DIARY or INTELLIGENCE SUMMARY.

Army Form C. 2118

(Erase heading not required.)

Hour, Date, Place	Summary of Events and Information	Remarks and references to Appendices
10 A.M. 5/8/14 ALDERSHOT	Reported and took over command of unit — Mobilization proceeding smoothly on existing establishment.	2nd day of Mobilization.
6/8/14	Following officers have joined — Lt Colonel J.C. MORGAN R.A.M.C. Commanding Major H.H. NORMAN " Major P.G. EASTON " Captain F. WORTHINGTON " Lieut C.S.H. MORSE S.R. Capt. & Q̇.m. R.R. COWAN. Captain CABLE joined and found medically unfit (S.R.)	3rd day of Mob. " " 4th day Mob.
7/8/14	Nothing special - Mobilization resumed	5th day Mob.
8/8/14	42 reservists joined	6th day Mob.
9/8/14	Lieut R.S.S. STATHAM Civil Surgeon joined	7th day Mob.
10/8/14	Captain A.R. DALE Civil Surgeon joined	8th day Mob.
11/8/14	Lieut E. WORDLEY Civil Surgeon joined	

WAR DIARY
or
INTELLIGENCE SUMMARY.
(Erase heading not required.)

Army Form C. 2118.

Instructions regarding War Diaries and Intelligence Summaries are contained in F.S. Regs., Part II. and the Staff Manual respectively. Title pages will be prepared in manuscript.

Hour, Date, Place	Summary of Events and Information	Remarks and references to Appendices
12/8/14 ALDERSHOT.	One R.A.M.C. officer, one baker + one A.S.E. reported to complete establishment. This wire buildup is complete & receiving is schedule of is very particular.	9th Day M.G. U.h.
13/8/14	Lieut. R.S. CLAUSEN R.E. joined for duty	10th Day M.G. U.h.
14/8/14	Building - Complete. Experting our buglar on a.s.c. Driver.	11th Day M.G. h.
15/8/14	Return held off and went exercised in outlying camp. Operated about an	12th " M.G. h.
16/8/14	heavy parade & others route march, spin field dressing demonstrations + lecture on T.R.A. etc.	13th " M.G. h.
17/9/14	As above. Instructions of Coys declined difficult to write.	14th " M.G. h.
18/8/14	march in trained in 2 baths fired party, cd.	15th " M.G. h.

Army Form C. 2118.

WAR DIARY
or
INTELLIGENCE SUMMARY.
(Erase heading not required.)

Instructions regarding War Diaries and Intelligence Summaries are contained in F.S. Regs., Part II. and the Staff Manual respectively. Title pages will be prepared in manuscript.

Hour, Date, Place	Summary of Events and Information	Remarks and references to Appendices
18/8/14 ALDERSHOT. Continued	First Parl. at 5.15 am. Next Parade decamping at 6.38 A.M. 6 Officers & 101 Men Free.	15th day Y/h
18/8/14 SOUTHAMPTON 10 A.M.	Went embarked all Complete (Canr S.S. wagons) in SS WELSHMAN – 8 S.S. wagons Shipped in SS ACHILBISTER – Sailed at 10. P.M. Same day. No casualties	15th Day Y/6 L
19/8/14 BOULOGNE 6.30 A.M.	Desembarked and proceeded to No. 1 Camp. MALBROOK. No casualties	16th Day Y/6 17th Day Y/6 L
20/8/14 BOULOGNE	In Camp. No casualties	
21/8/14 BOULOGNE	Marched out of Camp 5. P.M. and entrained at 6. P.M. No casualties - Train left at 10. P.M.	18" Y/6 L

WAR DIARY
or
INTELLIGENCE SUMMARY.
(Erase heading not required.)

Army Form C. 2118.

Hour, Date, Place	Summary of Events and Information	Remarks and references to Appendices
22/8/14 AULNOYE.	Detrained at 7. A.M. all complete. One horse lame and turned over to R.T.O. Provided by Make horsed at 3. P.M. for BEAUFORT via BACHANT and LIMONT FONTAINE.	J.G.
22/8/14 BEAUFORT	Arrived at 5.45. P.M. horsecoaches. Received orders from ADMS 1st Div to proceed to starting point LE PAVE & report to ADMS there at 7.30. P.M. — carried out & was dinner begun in behind No 1. F.A. & began to be turned out.	J.G.
23/8/14 GRAND RENG	Arrived at 2.45. A.M. Bivouaced. no Counterpan — billet allotted at 9. A.M.	J.G.

Army Form C. 2118.

WAR DIARY
or
INTELLIGENCE SUMMARY.

(*Erase heading not required.*)

Hour, Date, Place	Summary of Events and Information	Remarks and references to Appendices
23/8/14 7 p.m.	6th Cavalry Div'n Marched to & Crossroads 1 mi East of ELESMES and bivouacked Beaver Div'n prevented to ROUVEROY arriving escadrons	V.G.W.
24/8/14 5. a.m.	Just Div'n marched in return & was a about stoppage to rear weeks of 3rd/3rd Billethee or NEUF MESNIC for the night. Brun Subdiv'n rejoined at 9 p.m. to Cemetery 3 Sick one a cafe great opposition un transferred to the Red Cross hospice at HAUTMONT for operati- A.D.M.S. in support.	V.G.W.
25/8/14 5 a.m.	field ambulance backed to Neuf MESNIL returns to LE GRAND FAYT. now walking 10 officer & 28 men admitted sick including 3 cases gun shot wounds.	V.G.

Army Form C. 2118.

WAR DIARY
or
INTELLIGENCE SUMMARY.
(Erase heading not required.)

Instructions regarding War Diaries and Intelligence Summaries are contained in F.S. Regs., Part II. and the Staff Manual respectively. Title pages will be prepared in manuscript.

Hour, Date, Place	Summary of Events and Information	Remarks and references to Appendices
26/8/14 4 . . AM	No 3 F.A. Bn bearer Division moved the LE GRAND FAYT via PIECHES to ETRIEUX. Bearer division proceeded sick infirm by end of the 3rd Bayer to FAVRIL. Sick assembler lorry arr FAVRIL.	16 m
27/8/14 1 p.m.	Arrived at ETRIEUX and tent Division bivouacd – Bearer Division out with infantry units of J.	
27/8/14 10 . p.m	Bearer Division arrived with about 30 casualties in clouding one officer (Capt Shipway) wounded and one man dangerously wounded when the wagons reached ETRIEUX ted own sich bearer all accommodated in tents & houses surrounded in parts	bm

WAR DIARY
or
INTELLIGENCE SUMMARY.

Army Form C. 2118.

Hour, Date, Place	Summary of Events and Information	Remarks and references to Appendices
27/8/14 ETRIEUX	Captain Shipway died at 1.30 AM and was buried at ETRIEUX in the Catholic cemetery by the Revd. Blackburne. The men No 7856 Pt Sutherin of the 1st Glousters was also buried at the same time. Place by the Revd. Blackburne C of E Chaplain — 128 Sick wounded were evacuated by Train from ETRIEUX under the charge of Lt Honor R.A.M.C. S.R. The Engineer marched to BERNOT	ln ln
27/8/14 BERNOT 4 pm	The field ambulance billeted in a large farm. No casualties	

Army Form C. 2118.

WAR DIARY
or
INTELLIGENCE SUMMARY.
(Erase heading not required.)

Instructions regarding War Diaries and Intelligence Summaries are contained in F.S. Regs., Part II. and the Staff Manual respectively. Title pages will be prepared in manuscript.

Hour, Date, Place	Summary of Events and Information	Remarks and references to Appendices
BERNOT 3 AM 28/8/14	Field Ambulance marched at 3 a.m. to BERTANCOURT. 4 Casualties to 8 Sects. Arrived at about 1 p.m. & parked in an orchard.	—
BERTNCOURT 29/8/14 BERTAN COURT	To-day is a rest day. Cpl Bernard attached to the 12 Lancers was brought in wounded from headquarters to the Red Cross Hospital at St GOBAIN.	—

WAR DIARY
or
INTELLIGENCE SUMMARY.
(Erase heading not required.)

Army Form C. 2118.

Hour, Date, Place	Summary of Events and Information	Remarks and references to Appendices
BERTANCOURT 10. p.m 29/8/14	Tent the vini marched at 10pm via St GOBAIN and on the way the following cases were dropped at the CWC Red Cross Hospital at St GOBAIN— Sgt. Lumper Moulan 12" Lancers Pte. Croston 2/ Welch Pte. Griffiths 1/S.W.B. Pte. Murray R.F.a 54th By Henderson 3rd mounted. The ambulance entered some 1/2 an hour later stopped & their advance — in the movement The lines division recovered behind Fourcompany fighting & biga Jr	✓

Army Form C. 2118.

WAR DIARY
or
INTELLIGENCE SUMMARY.
(Erase heading not required.)

Hour, Date, Place	Summary of Events and Information	Remarks and references to Appendices
30/8/14 VAUX BUIN pres SOISSONS	The tent Div train arrived in camp about 4 p.m. The sick which we carried in the ambulances was all evacuated in train at SOISSONS railway station and in cluded the following officers — Captain Baynes of Gloucesters Lieut Gibson 2/ Welsh Regt — San throne Lieut Black w 1 in R.F.A. 1st Div Ammunition Column Fracture left forearm accidental	—

Army Form C. 2118.

WAR DIARY
or
INTELLIGENCE SUMMARY.
(Erase heading not required.)

Instructions regarding War Diaries and Intelligence Summaries are contained in F.S. Regs., Part II. and the Staff Manual respectively. Title pages will be prepared in manuscript.

Hour, Date, Place	Summary of Events and Information	Remarks and references to Appendices
31/8/14 VAUXBAIN pres SOISSONS	The tents & were bivouac during the night — the beam 2 were & in their regular. The tents during marched at 10 am for a brigade billet area.	
"		
MISSY LE BOIS	The tents & were huddle in a field in the rear of the main PARIS road near the village where the 18th is encamped. The beaver division reformed at 4 pm — having few wounded 5-3 cases and 1 suspect accident in the march.	

AMD

WAR DIARY.
No 3 Field Ambulance
Volume II.

WAR DIARY
or
INTELLIGENCE SUMMARY.

(Erase heading not required.)

Army Form C. 2118.

Instructions regarding War Diaries and Intelligence Summaries are contained in F. S. Regs., Part II. and the Staff Manual respectively. Title pages will be prepared in manuscript.

Hour, Date, Place	Summary of Events and Information	Remarks and references to Appendices
3/9/14 4. p.m. COULOMMIERS	For the past 48 hours the Field Ambulance has been employed in the march with but brief intervals for rest in [illegible]. From MISY-LE-BOIS the march was continued through MEAUX with a halt on the high ground at the S. [illegible] of the SAMS de [illegible] bivouacked 5 [illegible] in the [illegible] came to this morning, where it has been [illegible] a [illegible] on my [illegible] marched on to have been parked — until ordered to be expanded — the leave Division in the [illegible] being MISY LE BOIS. been detached	46

WAR DIARY
or
INTELLIGENCE SUMMARY.
(Erase heading not required.)

Army Form C. 2118.

Hour, Date, Place	Summary of Events and Information	Remarks and references to Appendices
4. p.m. 3/9/14 COULOMMIERS	and then been following the infantry and with 4 ambulance wagons. He stated I think the Ind [regiment?] wounded about 50 cases but no German soldiers — they are taken by some other [unit?] and taken in Rm Lorrain. Had tea in an Inn. The weather for the past [week?] has been extremely hot in the day time cold at night all sank an [?] except it has gone [quiet?] in seething in some town. Nothing but [?] under for one time an abundant but right up the times and it could not be [?] time	V.

Army Form C. 2118.

WAR DIARY
or
INTELLIGENCE SUMMARY.
(Erase heading not required.)

Instructions regarding War Diaries and Intelligence Summaries are contained in F.S. Regs., Part II. and the Staff Manual respectively. Title pages will be prepared in manuscript.

Hour, Date, Place	Summary of Events and Information	Remarks and references to Appendices
4/9/14 MOUROCN	The tent 2 division marched at 5 pm from the last camp arriving here at 10 pm. The packed all our men in a field. The leave division agreed at 1 pm with orders – orders you find but with Cavalerie holding Every tin.	N.L.
5/9/14 ROZOY 1 p.m.	The tent 2 division marched from — at 5 am their engaged by the rear guard. They were continued their march when the whole from 8.30 pm when the Cuirassic Spinden in afferir the Ridge y the MALPERTHUIS — ROZOY Road our 5th were them the back was covered by k. Company	N.L.

WAR DIARY
INTELLIGENCE SUMMARY.

(Erase heading not required.)

Army Form C. 2118.

Instructions regarding War Diaries and Intelligence Summaries are contained in F.S. Regs., Part II. and the Staff Manual respectively. Title pages will be prepared in manuscript.

Hour, Date, Place	Summary of Events and Information	Remarks and references to Appendices
Rozoy 5/9/14 1 P.m.	Continue to entrench the position which being must from 9 – 1. There are 3 several of British cavalry horses in the Australian in occupation of Rozoy. The beam Durgeon has arrived with the intention to work with 4 of the Australian squadrons & Units have no again in yet. There are no orders about.	6 m

Army Form C. 2118.

WAR DIARY
or
INTELLIGENCE SUMMARY.
(Erase heading not required.)

Instructions regarding War Diaries and Intelligence Summaries are contained in F.S. Regs., Part II. and the Staff Manual respectively. Title pages will be prepared in manuscript.

Hour, Date, Place	Summary of Events and Information	Remarks and references to Appendices
POMPIERRE 6/9/14	The tent I Wm. Larkin parked here are Oug. 15 wounded were received that afternoon & of these 5 were wounded above in 4 & one main body stabler in life on an Engineer's dressing station at PARADIS FARM to be evacuated later by motor lorries & young men. E.G.	

Army Form C. 2118.

WAR DIARY
or
INTELLIGENCE SUMMARY.
(Erase heading not required.)

Instructions regarding War Diaries and Intelligence Summaries are contained in F. S. Regs., Part II. and the Staff Manual respectively. Title pages will be prepared in manuscript.

Hour, Date, Place	Summary of Events and Information	Remarks and references to Appendices
7/9/14 VADDOY	2nd Division bivouaced at 7 p.m. last night traversed km at 12 midnight. Picked up stragglers who were killed in the day & were buried at VADDOY cemetery. The ug manus of inhabitants available showed that there were — artillery & suppressed & BOStein guns.	

Army Form C. 2118.

WAR DIARY
or
INTELLIGENCE SUMMARY.
(Erase heading not required.)

Instructions regarding War Diaries and Intelligence Summaries are contained in F.S. Regs., Part II. and the Staff Manual respectively. Title pages will be prepared in manuscript.

Hour, Date, Place	Summary of Events and Information	Remarks and references to Appendices
8/9/14 DAGNY 7 A.M.	First D wun marched at 2 p.m. from last camp yesterday + further then at 5 p.m. no casualties. Nothing special to note — 3 cases light in syphs sick were evacuated last evening. Special in progress. Bde becam division in strict with 3rd Inf.B R.F. Artyremy trib. no wounded.	L.

WAR DIARY
or
INTELLIGENCE SUMMARY.

(Erase heading not required.)

Army Form C. 2118

Hour, Date, Place	Summary of Events and Information	Remarks and references to Appendices
SABLONNIERE 9/9/14	First Division arrived here at 5 a.m. today. On DAY NY & our own OT suit was away from the transmit of No 1 Of this am 5 own Open the train. Germans Busket. 1 Officer Capt Dalglish 1/Black Watch & 1 man (Shore) Lt Gun report were brought there. The sick remaining were evacuated at 4. P.m. in motor lorries for rail head.	[signature]

WAR DIARY
or
INTELLIGENCE SUMMARY.
(Erase heading not required.)

Army Form C. 2118.

Hour, Date, Place	Summary of Events and Information	Remarks and references to Appendices
PRIEZ. 11/9/14 12 noon	1st Division marched from SABLONNIERES yesterday morning at 6.30 & arrived here at 10.15 p.m. last night. 10th Hussars 77 Casualties from W.I. Convoy Div. 6 Prisoners including one Officer(?) Knight of Royal Wurtembergers Regiment.) who is a prisoner here in 16 Cavalry Bgd. The enemy have here been ensconced from the ravines & railway cuts	[initials]

Army Form C. 2118.

WAR DIARY
or
INTELLIGENCE SUMMARY.
(Erase heading not required.)

Instructions regarding War Diaries and Intelligence Summaries are contained in F.S. Regs., Part II. and the Staff Manual respectively. Title pages will be prepared in manuscript.

Hour, Date, Place	Summary of Events and Information	Remarks and references to Appendices
LHUYS 12/9/14	1st Division marched from PRIEZ this morning and are bivouacked here tonight.	—
BOURG 13/9/14	2nd Division marched from LHUYS this morning and have bivouacked here tonight as usual.	—
BOURG 14/9/14	1st Division in Bourg area the station here this afternoon. Sick 17 cases hurts 2 Officers. These cases were left with a M.O. to be evacuated by motor lorries to the 1st Division bivouack at 8pm for VENDRESSE	—

WAR DIARY or INTELLIGENCE SUMMARY

Army Form C. 2118.

Hour, Date, Place	Summary of Events and Information	Remarks and references to Appendices
VENDRESSE 15/9/14	The Lieut Division arrived here from BOURG at 10 p.m. and took over some 300 wounded collected in buildings in the village – chiefly in the Chateau & Mairie – there were 16 Chateau & Mairie – there were also occasions spare cars were appropriated – 120 were evacuated at 11 a.m. to VILLERS and a further were evacuated at 6 p.m. The same place. The village has been heavily bombarded all day – there are three wounded German officers among them lying among wounded British officers.	

WAR DIARY
or
INTELLIGENCE SUMMARY.
(Erase heading not required.)

Army Form C. 2118.

Instructions regarding War Diaries and Intelligence Summaries are contained in F.S. Regs., Part II. and the Staff Manual respectively. Title pages will be prepared in manuscript.

Hour, Date, Place	Summary of Events and Information	Remarks and references to Appendices
VENDRESSE 16/9/14	The Stret Division & Bearer Division in the general subdivision are billetted in the Chateau & have evacuated from BEAUNE & SOUPIR & own sick evacuated from BEAUNE & CHIVY & VENDRESSE	
VENDRESSE 17/9/14	The work is about resuming established here & carrying sick over to base. Each night for VILLERS 90 men departed today	
VENDRESSE 18/9/14	1 Officer & 76 men evac. today. Evacuated to VILLERS. The area we have been having shells over today.	

Army Form C. 2118.

WAR DIARY
or
INTELLIGENCE SUMMARY.
(Erase heading not required.)

Hour, Date, Place	Summary of Events and Information	Remarks and references to Appendices
VILLERS 19/9/14	Orders were received at 8 p.m. last night for the 1st Div'n. one Bn. one Sqdn. & one Bty. of our Sub-division to remain at VILLERS & remainder to be attached to 1st Brigade. "B" Sqdn. was detailed at VENDRESSE with the remr. Div'n. "A" & "C" Sqdns. marched at 11.30pm to VILLERS arriving at 2.30am 75-Sick horses were evacuated with the CShans & the Remt. Divisions remained at VILLERS.	

Army Form C. 2118

WAR DIARY
or
INTELLIGENCE SUMMARY.
(Erase heading not required.)

Hour, Date, Place	Summary of Events and Information	Remarks and references to Appendices
VILLERS 20/9/14	A Convoy of S.S. Empty carts sent on to Vyers was despatched to Dunfte with a hurricane officer in company to VENDRESSE. It returned at 2.30 A.M. with 70 Sick & wounded N.C. which were transferred from 2 F.A. to waggons & sent back.	

Army Form C. 2118

WAR DIARY
or
INTELLIGENCE SUMMARY.
(Erase heading not required.)

Instructions regarding War Diaries and Intelligence Summaries are contained in F.S. Regs., Part II. and the Staff Manual respectively. Title pages will be prepared in manuscript.

Hour, Date, Place	Summary of Events and Information	Remarks and references to Appendices
21". 6. 23rd Sept 1914	The last Division is [further?] sent to a new position is now reported from VENDRESSE. Each regt. - a supply of tent [pegs?] [blankets?] & Shelters [given?] from [reserve?] & west of GUM 23/9 the two reserves & Distance - also 21 p.m. of fork to 100 Grey [Rails?] & 25[?] of [?] from [?] be performed.	V.G.h.
24th Sept	Situation unchanged without [?]	2G.h.
25th Sept	[?] unchanged [?] [?] troops	2G.h.
26th Sept	Situation unchanged without [?] troops [?]	2G.h.
	Enemy [?] over [?] in [?]	

WAR DIARY
or
INTELLIGENCE SUMMARY.
(Erase heading not required.)

Army Form C. 2118

Instructions regarding War Diaries and Intelligence Summaries are contained in F. S. Regs., Part II. and the Staff Manual respectively. Title pages will be prepared in manuscript.

Hour, Date, Place	Summary of Events and Information	Remarks and references to Appendices
Febr. 29. VILLERS	Lt. Col. Morgan having received orders to proceed at once to take over No 2. Equine Hospital, he left at 12.30 p.m. & handed over the command to Lieut. Sellon Pearce. Orders received later 15/3/06 No 2 F.A. from No. M.D.M.S. 1st Div. Capt. Dunton VENDRESSE 10/2 returned with a convoy of wounded & reported his arrival to O.C. No 2. F.O. Ho.	Re Each Make Name
	Intertan movements. Equip & Horses Op. Dir. on board	Pss
	equipment – 200 Blankets. 3000 Lbs. Biscuits 100 A Bandage as No. Caldera Pass–	PS
Sept 29. 30.	Sent one draught of 3 Field Ambulances. Repairs night to horses.	Arthayne horse Arm

14/18/15
Dec 1914

S/ Co 3 Field Ambulance

Vol VII

Army Form C. 2118.

WAR DIARY
or
INTELLIGENCE SUMMARY.
(Erase heading not required.)

Instructions regarding War Diaries and Intelligence Summaries are contained in F. S. Regs., Part II. and the Staff Manual respectively. Title pages will be prepared in manuscript.

Hour, Date, Place	Summary of Events and Information	Remarks and references to Appendices
Oct 2 Villers	Trains arrived drawing station at Vauxrot. Brought back horses belonging to 7 A & Section not reported late. B section horses this morning 05th inst.	Authority ref.
Oct 14	21 horse entrained 15 Issaet (Transferred to 2 Div.)	Ann
Oct 15	Left Villers at 11.30 pm and marched to Braisne as a F.A.	Ann
	10 miles from Braisne to Neuilly St Front where entrained for Etaples + thence to St Omer 18.15	
Oct 18	Marched 15 Strazeele to Gds 19.15	Ann
Oct 20	While Field Ambulance marched on to Poperinghe and at 3.45 am went on to Elverdinghe where we were billeted.	
Oct 21	Proceeding towards Langemarck today the 3rd Brigade became engaged with the enemy & the 6th Divison eventually to Westreve. Officers + 18 Stretcher & O.S. Wagons and a Water Cart formed a dressing station	

WAR DIARY or INTELLIGENCE SUMMARY

Army Form C. 2118.

Instructions regarding War Diaries and Intelligence Summaries are contained in F.S. Regs., Part II. and the Staff Manual respectively. Title pages will be prepared in manuscript.

(Erase heading not required.)

Hour, Date, Place	Summary of Events and Information	Remarks and references to Appendices
Oct 22.	at Farm BOSSAERT — 1/2 mile S. of 1st village. Troops sending an advanced dressing station to the rear. Found to be Westroosebeke. Buildings at the side of the rear of Keyem Battery last night. Shelling our lorries through morning. The advanced dressing station were withdrawn. A large number of wounded were treated at the farm, & stretcher bearers were sent to search certain areas, in order to let to leave. Certain Canon. Evacuation was by army wounded men. Ambulance wagons at lights.	
Oct 23.	We still continued to the FARM BOSSAERT as a dressing station today. Oct 22 and 250 wounded have passed through. Here 3 dead & 7 men have been buried in a bunch.	

79/3298

WAR DIARY
or
INTELLIGENCE SUMMARY.
(Erase heading not required.)

Army Form C. 2118.

Hour, Date, Place	Summary of Events and Information	Remarks and references to Appendices
Oct 24	Fred at the house of the farmer. Moved on by night to Ypres via the 95th, stayed at Hall 6 in Poor billets.	
25	The Bosche shells were presented at the morning on a Brigade with the expectation of meeting the enemy. The 7th Division was the first offs to make the Division enduring shells at ECOLE BIENFAISANT a very satisfactory place for the purpose in YPRES. We were prepared very far looking not of the day but firing in front. In the evening the horse division were billeted at a Chateau.	
26.		
27.	Followed the 3rd Brigade there asked to form a screen at the Q & GLENCORSE with the hope by Brigade Major. This proved to be an unsuitable place to open, & 2 lecturer officers & all the transport were sent	

WAR DIARY
or
INTELLIGENCE SUMMARY.

(Erase heading not required.)

Army Form C. 2118.

Hour, Date, Place	Summary of Events and Information	Remarks and references to Appendices
	Away & forth had under cover. A' Section remained in one of our to trenches, Sheldon parties under the Coy. & Coy. M's into trenches into intermittently overhead shelling. We buried M.s & more killed. 3 men who were inside of the time. Their names were Pte. Morgan, Pte. Bailey & Pte Perry R.A.M.C. There was a good deal of sniping, Stolen established by MO! F.A. close to this spot, no room for other wires 16th Rangers were, so in connection with Col. Inigo a section of bearers, & the R.F.C. were to work out + 2 M.O's were left to [...] the stretcher withdrawn to the Divisional Collecting Station. My Ambulance wagons have also [...] at [...] Huiges dispersed. The are about 80 wounded men in [hospital] the Convent [...] tonight to there.	ahoe

WAR DIARY
or
INTELLIGENCE SUMMARY.
(Erase heading not required.)

Army Form C. 2118.

Hour, Date, Place	Summary of Events and Information	Remarks and references to Appendices
Oct 28th	During today numerous things were done to made the wounded & sick transport with a suitable divisional collecting station. The number of patients are greatly increasing. The orderlies were most obliging & have to lending with advice and pulling their work with our outpost. The wounded are brought to Chicken at our outpost. US there where the Mess have their house. Taken to 13 from with another carrier where a motor ambce is sent by the R.? Blackburn Res. on to the Divn. O. One have now 1st for days some enemy aircraft for times each. Total number for eight even. to lemon wounded makes develop out Evacuation of the wounded represents. Such a large number of patients my nervous. Previous he is now my first orderly. I with drew my advanced dressing Station forward	
29th		

WAR DIARY
or
INTELLIGENCE SUMMARY.
(Erase heading not required.)

Army Form C. 2118.

Hour, Date, Place	Summary of Events and Information	Remarks and references to Appendices
30.	and for urgent cases; so before my ambulance began work, O.C. from F.A. As the men arrived, motor ambulance began take then to the train, & there has been no correspondence difficulty in treating patients. Plenty of food is to be obtained, & the water supply is satisfactory.	
31	Today the number of sick, some 6 to 20. In the A.F.A. came orders to proceed to a point not for from a certain line no wounded have found, having been the first time no wounded were to a very late period(?) evacuated by some one else. Wounds have been to have been fit to lived in a very late period(?) boy to evacuating stations. Considering the difficulty that conditions exist in this weather, and I have been have who are exhausted from exposure of want of food remain.	

12/2/14
Mar. 19th

ANO

S/

Co 3. Field Ambulance.

Vol IV.

No. 3 Fld. Amb. Army Form C. 2118.

WAR DIARY
or
INTELLIGENCE SUMMARY.
(Erase heading not required.)

Hour, Date, Place	Summary of Events and Information	Remarks and references to Appendices
Nov. 1st	Owing to the number of wounded entered here this afternoon we had to close down & send on patients elsewhere. Engaged in during the rest of the day in evacuating sick and by midnight 1-2 Nov. all settling up were sent to away.	Clear & warm.
Nov 2.	This morning we have down to 40 patients. The majority of the wounded have been evacuated. Kind in helping in every possible way.	Clear.
Nov 3	We have been to very busy here since last nite. The number who have brought here from the wounded amounts to over 300. Since we first opened the business has continued clearing station it has been because the most advanced clearing station by the progress of the engagement. The wounded have in large numbers come here	Clear.

Army Form C. 2118.

WAR DIARY
or
INTELLIGENCE SUMMARY.
(Erase heading not required.)

Instructions regarding War Diaries and Intelligence Summaries are contained in F.S. Regs., Part II. and the Staff Manual respectively. Title pages will be prepared in manuscript.

Hour, Date, Place	Summary of Events and Information	Remarks and references to Appendices
	What exists a enemies attn moment Hits a work + arrangement. Rope shells fire close together. The stables + coach'n horse. The floor windows most have also been slightly damaged too. Arrangements have been made for hire line for temporary Patients for the cellars which have been placed.	Awkward [?]
YPRES. 16.10.14.	Orders to have emergencies battery of R.A. rep at 8.40 P.M. S 39' batteries have been linked at 10 L'cow Provitor and by us during it last Brought.	Own
LO eRÉ. 17.11.14.	arrived here 3. a.m. + Breakfast in a form in the afternoon + 2 h.h. m kinetics to OULTERSTEEN. stage the canvas also 8.30. P.M.	
OULTERSTEEN. 11.14.	Busted in school here and two horses. Quarters again in this opposite	Own

Army Form C. 2118.

WAR DIARY
or
INTELLIGENCE SUMMARY.
(Erase heading not required.)

Instructions regarding War Diaries and Intelligence Summaries are contained in F.S. Regs., Part II. and the Staff Manual respectively. Title pages will be prepared in manuscript.

Hour, Date, Place	Summary of Events and Information	Remarks and references to Appendices
OOTHERSTEEN Nov. 19th	There was snow last night + frost. Orders the riding horses could be put in the carts. Six Men of F.A. here given 96 hours leave to proceed to England (and draw pay for from the proposits.	Murphy
Nov. 20	Considerable frost last night. Paid the men this morning. Brins. 250 Paid n.l. 2250 = Cost Brins. 2000 2250	Own
Nov. 21	In hand nil. Proceeded to Eighne on 5 days leave, leaving Major Eaton in charge. There were two lorries Church weekly against them, one for rations + heating into advance, and one (A.S.C.) for rations and and one in the A.S.C.	Own
Nov. 28.	Returning from leave took over charge of F.A again.	Own

Endersough

No 3 Field Ambulance.

Vol I.

12/1307
Dec 1914

Army Form C. 2118.

WAR DIARY
or
INTELLIGENCE SUMMARY.
(Erase heading not required.)

Instructions regarding War Diaries and Intelligence Summaries are contained in F. S. Regs., Part II. and the Staff Manual respectively. Title pages will be prepared in manuscript.

Hour, Date, Place	Summary of Events and Information	Remarks and references to Appendices
Dec. 1st	Changed 1st Fused in which the troops are now here in reserve of front. at 12.5. the men reported of No 3 were paraded for an inspection by his Grace of Such. Br. Rawup in the shape of a speech the C in C addressed them. He referred to the fine work of the Rawls in the war, and spoke of the hardships done at YPRES by the unit.	Anthrope
Dec 2nd	A quiet day. Officers' attention has been drawn to all little homes in which the N.C.Os. officers and little Officers observe the horses are in from evolution. In the evening a successful concert was given by the men, and attended by the Officers	

Army Form C. 2118.

WAR DIARY
or
INTELLIGENCE SUMMARY.
(Erase heading not required.)

Instructions regarding War Diaries and Intelligence Summaries are contained in F.S. Regs., Part II. and the Staff Manual respectively. Title pages will be prepared in manuscript.

Hour, Date, Place	Summary of Events and Information	Remarks and references to Appendices
June 3rd METEREN	Yesterday 15 Officers and men prisoners were brought to the Cage. Roads in return to METEREN for an inspection by the Deputy Recruiting. The King passes between thousands drawn up by the roads. This Church was free for him to be bombed along the lines.	Autograph
June 10th	Today we received 14 Belgian infantry in exchange for 4 hussars which we returned to STAVEELE Siding. Lt. SYKES amused the men he keeping fit. We met mostly proper cheese and football. Two hundred enemy have been hurt.	
June 30th	Left GUTERSTEEN to BETHUNE (at Cressy). The battalion at billets for 3 hours at Mc.GUIRE	

Army Form C. 2118.

WAR DIARY
or
INTELLIGENCE SUMMARY.
(Erase heading not required.)

Instructions regarding War Diaries and Intelligence Summaries are contained in F.S. Regs., Part II. and the Staff Manual respectively. Title pages will be prepared in manuscript.

Hour, Date, Place	Summary of Events and Information	Remarks and references to Appendices
Dec. 21st	Renewed RETIRE but did not stop firing an advance from 3rd Brigade via LE QUESNOY being	Authorities
22nd	We stopped the nights march. The 3rd Brigade being now in action round LE BURET headquarters and arrived Le Coke on CHATEAU GORRE as 1st F.A. or advanced Division area.	
23rd	On the night of 22-23rd there was a considerable and the enemy and enemy into the trenches by night which the men had become accustomed to the trenches put a certainty of fires obtained at the front into this trench and to probable losses Holding their own and to probable losses. The General Call & promise to Bde.	
24th	Again a quiet night. One of the above but four hours. Bde CHATEAU GORRE in working order	

WAR DIARY or INTELLIGENCE SUMMARY

Army Form C. 2118.

(Erase heading not required.)

Hour, Date, Place	Summary of Events and Information	Remarks and references to Appendices
Wed 27	Brutus Arrived, left 15 Chelsea to look to the Services Vaast where he was superintending hospital and also a hospital train.	ambulance
28	Left SENINGHEM VAAST [?] Tor F.A. and met 15 EGUE JEUVES C & Crews. 15 [...] by F.A. (12th Division)	Leave officer Leave. do
29	Early days known at le CHÂTEAU GORRE, 6 look serving the [...] station was shelled and manettes w 15 dept of PUIBRICH As C. & 15 wounding of Driver Clements A.S.C. A horse was also wounded and a motor ambulance damaged.	
31st	He hereis remained at GORRE but [...] about 15 villages to GIVID against 15 [dangers] of shell-fire as to [provide] Patients are less to go to No. 1 F.A. as Bevry for 15 present, as it is convenient	

WAR DIARY
or
INTELLIGENCE SUMMARY.
(Erase heading not required.)

Army Form C. 2118.

Hour, Date, Place	Summary of Events and Information	Remarks and references to Appendices
Béthune 31st Dec 1914	Having to billet them with on Chateau — if it can be arranged for the present. dep.r Ests received while G.O.C. to H.Q.G. 1st Corps and Lt. Yates 2nd i/c and Lt. Clemens have been transferred from No 3 F.A. to be in the [?] Sussex 16 Regt.	Ann bridge [?]

Ans

No 3. Field Ambulance.

Vol VI.

12/4257
Jan 19/15.

Jan to July 31st

Army Form C.2118.

3rd Field Ambulance

WAR DIARY
or
INTELLIGENCE SUMMARY.

(Erase heading not required.)

Instructions regarding War Diaries and Intelligence Summaries are contained in F.S. Regs., Part II. and the Staff Manual respectively. Title pages will be prepared in manuscript.

Hour, Date, Place	Summary of Events and Information	Remarks and references to Appendices
Jan? 1st 1915. Bethune.	The War Diary puts the Unit "en billets" at L'Eure Jeune Garcons" and the Brer division at CHATEAU GOSNÉ where they bring in the Sick and wounded from the 3rd Brigade at FESUBERT. After being Seen to, the men are sent on Stretchers to No 1 F.A. at BÉUVRY, as it is generally safe to allow them to remain in the CHATEAU for long on account of shelling. For the same reason the men of the bearer Co are being billeted in houses around the building rather than in it, building itself.	All hopes up
Jan 8.15	The bearers were ordered by the A.D.M.S who had been withdrawn Bethune, the 3rd Brigade has been leaving, a sheer truck This officer from just before leaving, near the Croix Rouge Calais home on one coming?	Aunt Hope

WAR DIARY
or
INTELLIGENCE SUMMARY.
(*Erase heading not required.*)

Army Form C. 2118.

Hour, Date, Place	Summary of Events and Information	Remarks and references to Appendices
BETHUNE Jan 10th	To a Mountain battery	Authority
11th	to ascertain from 1st Field Ambulance Disposition of 1st Advance. On return seen hospital by 1st Advance. On return seen hospital arrangements. The four mls. from 15th Divisions to No 6 F.A. in Bethune.	
12	4 four four to 1st R. Irish Fusiliers and Cpl Acheson ? in his place.	
14th	The R.I. Smith Regan proceeds to the line at Haisnes.	
15th	The trench ditches & ? det'n? for our to BEUVRY to take over the arrangement Station was taken by Major F.A. his horses fires in Gutram command C. No 2 F.A.	
16	Major ? with ? command of	Authority

WAR DIARY
or
INTELLIGENCE SUMMARY.

(Erase heading not required.)

Army Form C.2118.

Hour, Date, Place	Summary of Events and Information	Remarks and references to Appendices
BEUVRY. Jan 16th	The Col Allison & transport in Bethune at the Ecole des frères Garçons. Capt Davis & Capt Doyle's Essex also remain. The Regt Aid Post & Lt Fotheringham are billeted in BEUVRY and a small HQ. learn to an advanced dressing station in front of the Square at a house known as "The Chateau". We keep one motor ambulance always on duty, night & day. One horse ambce. Its Reserve and horse Ambulance for it. Its errand the men of Two Brigades which is a duty we find it hard to cope with.	Anthon[?] [sig]

WAR DIARY
or
INTELLIGENCE SUMMARY.
(Erase heading not required.)

Army Form C. 2118.

Hour, Date, Place	Summary of Events and Information	Remarks and references to Appendices
BEUVRY Jan 17	U. Wright/sm. The fred Antlaine -	
25th	This morning 15th in are attacked by the Germans and some fighting. We were over/pds all 15th and were 6.30 a.m. the 26th in Billy is bombed, shewing the and wounded there. Army left Division and all its hospital here ordered away.	
6.15 orders see p. Bethune to 15th Div land down Station had gone 470 miles here to dink out, and bivouac had now two fragments of Germans tied near too.	
26th	that than to CHOQUES and LILLERS. Kaw birthday + back to BETHUNE	Anthony m

WAR DIARY or INTELLIGENCE SUMMARY.

Army Form C. 2118.

(Erase heading not required.)

Hour, Date, Place	Summary of Events and Information	Remarks and references to Appendices
Bethune. Jan. 28th	to take over the work of the (and 9th) Military Hospital set by the 7th Division. Sick tone in division rifts at BEUVRY. the No. 1 F.A. is BETHUNE and wounded were to be at the civil + military hospital BETHUNE.	
Jan. 29	Sick huts opened F.A. as ambulance to work between BEUVRY and 7 Divs in the Civil + military hospital lay on motors work between the two BEUVRY.	
Jan. 31st	Major BEUVRY today on a foot down up firing end of the road. Brought in Capt Whittington & Lt Ainsley to help us in BETHUNE also some lorries.	

121/4657

121/4657
Dec 19.1915

3rd Field Ambulance

Vol VII

Ans.

WAR DIARY
or
INTELLIGENCE SUMMARY.
(Erase heading not required.)

Army Form C. 2118.

Hour, Date, Place	Summary of Events and Information	Remarks and references to Appendices
BETHUNE Feb 1st 1915.	The Attached dressing Station is out at BEUVRY but closed pending a move. The Indian division is working Civil & Military hospital, taking both wounded & sick men. We have our own F.A. having closed down from two wilh beds etc & 2 wards with four and two with beds etc & 2 wards. Two operating rooms, multiroom on the floor.	
Feby 3rd	No 4 Field Ambulance came and relieved the 1st division at the Civil & Militim hospital BETHUNE. The Perou division out at BEUVRY (which is really the leave district) are orders to join up with by the 1st (our own at 1 overua) the whole Field Ambulance No 3. moved out to LABEUVRIÈRE. There be are billeted in a large building late Chunck altered. Only quarters for the been are in the	Weather etc Very heavy

Army Form C. 2118.

WAR DIARY
or
INTELLIGENCE SUMMARY.
(Erase heading not required.)

Instructions regarding War Diaries and Intelligence Summaries are contained in F.S. Regs., Part II. and the Staff Manual respectively. Title pages will be prepared in manuscript.

Hour, Date, Place	Summary of Events and Information	Remarks and references to Appendices
LA BEUVRIÈRE		
Feb 4th	action, and no satisfactory place exist for horses. General cleaning up of billets, & attention to sanitary matters.	
Feb 5th	We are ordered to open up washing arrangements for the Brigade at the Baths allotted to a coal mine at BRUAY. Here the one 64 shower baths, clean washing is obtained from No. 1 F.A. and dirty linen is taken away by D.E. Train deciding a cart for the purpose.	
Feb 6th	Difficulty in obtaining clean underclothing to what has not been let to be bought. A Chiropodist is sent for cutting nails, some from is proved to hurt, and petrol for brushing the woods of men's trousers too. A few horses being sick, any clean	Continued on

Army Form C.2118.

WAR DIARY
or
INTELLIGENCE SUMMARY.

(Erase heading not required.)

Instructions regarding War Diaries and Intelligence Summaries are contained in F.S. Regs., Part II. and the Staff Manual respectively. Title pages will be prepared in manuscript.

Hour, Date, Place	Summary of Events and Information	Remarks and references to Appendices
LA BOUVRIÈRE	To be knocked at night to take one of clocks requirements.	
Feb 7th	Leave is again granted for 6 days. Major Norman proceeds home. Capt O'Neill R? Cameron dit?	
Feb 10th	Lt Gunning is sent to R.F.A 1st Canadian div. Lt Sykes to 1st London Section. Lt Wright to the Inner Water Bordure.	
Feb 13th	A party of new entrants to be last drink to the Battery. Establishment under are Other Ranks horses + drill to keep the men fit. Proceed on leave. Major Norman came over	
Feb 15	Charge.	
Feb 23	Returned from leave to England. T.A. still in LA BOUVRIÈRE.	Arthur for Lt Col.

WAR DIARY
or
INTELLIGENCE SUMMARY.

Army Form C. 2118.

(Erase heading not required.)

Hour, Date, Place	Summary of Events and Information	Remarks and references to Appendices
LA BOUVRIERE Feb 25.	Receive orders to send 4 heavy and 4 medium Offrs to ESSARS to deal with 3rd Brigade now proceeding to the area. Paris leave notes now stopped.	
Feb 26.	Visited the hutts at BRUAY. Afternoon wet. Lt BROME visited my new area to learn for a place for establishing my F.A.	
Feb 27th	Receive orders to march to BETHUNE and later on ECOLE MICHELET. Baths house. With me G.T. No 1 F.A. at BRUAY.	
Feb 28th Bethune	Settled in to ECOLE MICHELET. and Offrs may go for baths. Motor ambulance lorries are arriving at a point near J.T.U.B.E 85 for 3rd Brigade Such wounded, and men ESSARS for the 1st Brigade Div. One Offr and 3 Motor Lorries are kept at	Authority Lt.Col. Rome

Army Form C.2118.

WAR DIARY
or
INTELLIGENCE SUMMARY.

(Erase heading not required.)

Instructions regarding War Diaries and Intelligence Summaries are contained in F.S. Regs., Part II. and the Staff Manual respectively. Title pages will be prepared in manuscript.

Hour, Date, Place	Summary of Events and Information	Remarks and references to Appendices
BETHUNE. 3rd John	E.S.A.R.S. + three visit the first aid posts in the Rue du Brie + Rue de l'Epinette. In the basement was a motor ambulance as at its lowered turning for at Festubert, where 2 stretcher squads + one officer being in great demands from the aid posts about here.	Air Marshn in Ch Rome.

121/4801

12/4807
March 1915

No 3. Field Ambulance

Vol VIII

WAR DIARY
or
INTELLIGENCE SUMMARY.

(Erase heading not required.)

Army Form C. 2118.

Hour, Date, Place	Summary of Events and Information	Remarks and references to Appendices
BETHUNE March 1st 1915.	The F.A. is distributed as follows. (1) One Officer and 3 motor ambulances plus 3 studebaker cars at ESQUARS. (2) 1 Officer 2 motor ambulances and 2 studebakers at FESTUBERT. The whole under Major Dorman Rourke.	
March 4.	Remainder of French Ambulance at ECOLE MICHELET forming a hospital of about 150 beds. The nature of their work is at present one of chance. The nature of their and leaves at 16 but are changes + this is to be a weekly affair.	
March 9th	Received orders to transfer ECOLE MICHELET and proceed to ECOLE BERT and make a hospital	(Signed) Ll. Col.

Army Form C. 2118.

WAR DIARY
or
INTELLIGENCE SUMMARY.
(Erase heading not required.)

Instructions regarding War Diaries and Intelligence Summaries are contained in F. S. Regs., Part II. and the Staff Manual respectively. Title pages will be prepared in manuscript.

Hour, Date, Place	Summary of Events and Information	Remarks and references to Appendices
Feb.	There was not so much bombing and MG fire found for [?] near Elsewhere. The O.F.C. trumpet-blowers were left behind in H.Q. and here, no state has been anywhere Elsewhere. The distance away is under a mile.	
Feb 10th	The Battle of Neuve Chapelle today — also at GIVENCHY. 1st Division has much engaged and we had no great number of wounded from our area. Lt. Corcoran killed by C.M. for drunkenness when doing trumpery regimental duty with the British regiment.	
Feb 15.		
Feb 18.	An extra number of planes went out this morning in anticipation of fighting, but nothing out of the way occurred.	Autopsy over

WAR DIARY
or
INTELLIGENCE SUMMARY.
(Erase heading not required.)

Army Form C. 2118.

Hour, Date, Place	Summary of Events and Information	Remarks and references to Appendices
Feb 19	Lt Montgomery goes to LOUVEN duty to the Plant	
	refine (shequently remains so permanent attached).	
	The horses at FESTUBERT and ESSARS are	
	relieved by No 2 F.A and come in to PAUL IBERT.	
Feb 20	Lt WRIGHT & Lt SYKES go on leave to England.	
Feb 22	Lt CORCORAN dis honoured His Majesty's Service	
	leaves for England.	
	Two sections of horses under L.C.R Norman proceed	
March 24	to LA COUTURE to take over the NEUVE	
	CHAPPELLE area for collecting in. Patrols on	
	bright were by two roads, to LACOUTURE	
	(where the detachment is billeted) and to	
	the only LATOURET & BETHUNE.	Anthony
	One note advance screen - Penaissance by not	is en.

Army Form C. 2118.

WAR DIARY
or
INTELLIGENCE SUMMARY.
(Erase heading not required.)

Instructions regarding War Diaries and Intelligence Summaries are contained in F.S. Regs., Part II. and the Staff Manual respectively. Title pages will be prepared in manuscript.

Hour, Date, Place	Summary of Events and Information	Remarks and references to Appendices
	On the ESTAIRES – LA BASSÉE main road (sheltered by a cottage) for being enemy myself kept constantly from NEUVE CHAPELLE way. The wounds are not however from this. 10 – 20 daily. Priv. Woodhouse A.S.C. the Divr (Farm) is last day we were at KMBOURIÈRES bro near Saive reported.	
March 25.	He & a & trumpet have been hurs from the Tabla to R.O.B. M'CHELET to the presence of the cracker much in BOULEVARD THIERS.	
March 27.	to Young Jim to feed Andrews, & to Cleaner from the floors returns to me.	
Feb 28.	Paid arrived to LA COUTURE and now to	Autograph D.C.A.

Army Form C. 2118.

WAR DIARY
or
INTELLIGENCE SUMMARY.
(Erase heading not required.)

Hour, Date, Place	Summary of Events and Information	Remarks and references to Appendices
March 31st	the first aid parts of 3rd Brigade. Relief of one section of lewis guns by Captain also Capt. O'Neil and 16 lewis Gunners - also Capt. O'Neil and 16 others two men Private - Clancey One pte. Phelan away by men he remains One sling knee sent to Hoss. GLEESON hurt with the Municks Fusiliers.	Authorgr of Co.

121/5/61

12/5/61
April 1915

No 3 Field Ambulance

Vol IX

Army Form C. 2118.

WAR DIARY
or
INTELLIGENCE SUMMARY.
(Erase heading not required.)

Hour, Date, Place	Summary of Events and Information	Remarks and references to Appendices
1915. April 1st BETHUNE	Been division from NEUVE CHAPELLE area. Tent division open at ECOLE PAUL BERT. Still.	
April 2.	Driving the canal of the day. I visited the house division at La COUTURE, and also a post where we keep a motor ambulance for running temp(orar)y cases at NEUVE CHAPELLE. From this post to the 1st Aid posts near this is a light railway — (trolley + wooden rails) which runs all the way. Stretcher cases in this part to places on a trolley + pushed down with front rope.	Arthur U.CR. Reeve

Army Form C. 2118.

WAR DIARY
or
INTELLIGENCE SUMMARY.
(Erase heading not required.)

Instructions regarding War Diaries and Intelligence Summaries are contained in F. S. Regs., Part II. and the Staff Manual respectively. Title pages will be prepared in manuscript.

Hour, Date, Place	Summary of Events and Information	Remarks and references to Appendices
April 5th	The Point of Maxim was given to the officers at LA COUTURE by the Rev. Mr. Blackburn. An inspection after hours by Captain Mulgrew and the Veterinary Officer has been held, and both are pleased with their condition. The is partly due to Sergeant Weller who has himself spent a lot of time in clipping horses and improved the look of his platoon.	
April 6th	L. Cpl. Norman left the Field Ambulance on the 3rd to take over charge of troops Canadian Clearing hospital.	Authorper Lt Col R Caine

Army Form C. 2118.

WAR DIARY
or
INTELLIGENCE SUMMARY.
(Erase heading not required.)

Instructions regarding War Diaries and Intelligence Summaries are contained in F.S. Regs., Part II. and the Staff Manual respectively. Title pages will be prepared in manuscript.

Hour, Date, Place	Summary of Events and Information	Remarks and references to Appendices
April 7th	Today in relief of the 2nd Brigade, the horse pack trains are ordered to return to BETHUNE. Captain O'Neill has been in charge of them during the week.	
April 16th	The dogs who have not come forward for inoculation through Eclaise [?] from here declined today to [illegible].	
April 17th	Sent me new A.S.C. [?] horse & mule animal ambulance drivers have increased to 07. At 12 m. say two subdivisions of horses & mule ambulances & one horse wagon [proceeded] to LATOURET[?] Authorpe[?] et al. Rain	

(D 26 6) W 257—976 100,000 4/12 H WV 79/3298

WAR DIARY
or
INTELLIGENCE SUMMARY.
(Erase heading not required.)

Army Form C. 2118.

Hour, Date, Place	Summary of Events and Information	Remarks and references to Appendices
April 18th	Under Captain Mackay the following men, including 15 Rue des Bois, 15 Rue de l'Epinette and RICHEBOURG (for the 3rd Brigade) went out last night.	
	[illegible lines]	
	At night 10 sent to 15th R, number taken to make the regiment - vice 1 Captain the Colonel reporting.	
April 19th	Lt. McCaul, 1st to the 1st Auxiliary	
April 21	Lt. Parr to 15th Field Ambulance.	Authorized West

Army Form C. 2118.

WAR DIARY
or
INTELLIGENCE SUMMARY.
(Erase heading not required.)

Hour, Date, Place	Summary of Events and Information	Remarks and references to Appendices
April 25th	The trains Division returned to BETHUNE in relief by No 2 F.A. – During the time at LE TOURET there were not a great many wounded here. The last division column seen here.	
April 27.	A Imperial Indian detachment to fit MT convoy by 19 R.F. Ambulances in its depot	
April 29.	Lt Life proceed to form an Ambulance train. Lt Bew will have to exchange ?	
April 30.	The horses and harness at the starting had grown very much interested by cart holding and have found satisfactory	

Anthony
O. C.

121/5513

121/5513

1st Division

No 3. Field Ambulance

Pt X

May 1915

Army Form C. 2118.

WAR DIARY
or
INTELLIGENCE SUMMARY.
(Erase heading not required.)

Instructions regarding War Diaries and Intelligence Summaries are contained in F.S. Regs., Part II. and the Staff Manual respectively. Title pages will be prepared in manuscript.

Hour, Date, Place	Summary of Events and Information	Remarks and references to Appendices
BETHUNE May 1st 1915.	Whole Ambulance returned at ECOLE Paul Bert.	
BETHUNE May 2.	The men were marched to HINGETTE and Church parade by the Rev. Mr. Polwarthian.	
May 3.	A lecture was given by O.C. F.A. on the health of the men and Stretcher Bearers in case of a new casing place.	
May 4.	A practical demonstration of the lecture given yesterday.	
May 5.	Stretcher squads again exercised in removing (carrying) for removal of wounded men.	

Aus Hooper
Lt. Col.

WAR DIARY
or
INTELLIGENCE SUMMARY.
(Erase heading not required.)

Army Form C. 2118.

Hour, Date, Place	Summary of Events and Information	Remarks and references to Appendices
BETHUNE May 6.15 May 7.	A lecture was given to the men today on Return to the field by Capt. O'Neill. All stretcher bearers under Capt. Worthington proceeded to LA COUTURE where an advanced dressing station was prepared. The CO. & the Rev. Mr ?? have bivouacked. The ?? Blackburn also remains here. One of the ambulance wagons has been fitted with a lamp operating & generally arranged for running up to an advanced position where no ?? wounded of dressing cases were evident. This does not of course extend that the Coy. cannot be utilised for its purpose of carrying.	Worthington 4 C.A.

WAR DIARY
or
INTELLIGENCE SUMMARY

Army Form C. 2118.

Hour, Date, Place	Summary of Events and Information	Remarks and references to Appendices
BETHUNE May 8th	Wounds men of 2 weeks. The horses count was favorably improved today & an action being expected towards Capt Lumley(?) went forward to one of the head front so an observation officer with our cyclists. He is able to keep us informed as to the condition of affairs in front as far as our troops & concerned, & it was the difficult to offer experienced officers Cavalry unit front out posts during the day of an action.	
May 9th	A Battle took place in which we took horses and the allied arms a great much of casualties. [strikethrough] We were employed	[illegible]

WAR DIARY
or
INTELLIGENCE SUMMARY

(Erase heading not required.)

Army Form C. 2118.

Hour, Date, Place	Summary of Events and Information	Remarks and references to Appendices
BETHUNE	is bringing men in, sends out motor Shunters & stretcher bearers, he some motor Ambulances were not allowed up. The stretcher bearers worked with great energy & determination. At about 3.15 p.m. a fresh attack was made with all great result as far as casualties were concerned. The bearers had therefore to be employed & Capt. Keogh again kept his motor Ambulances from No. 101 bearers & more motor Cars were sent up.	
May 10th	After collecting all last night, at 2 a.m. there were no wounded left to be removed as far as one knew. The men were	As before to OC 1.

WAR DIARY
or
INTELLIGENCE SUMMARY

(Erase heading not required.)

Army Form C. 2118.

Hour, Date, Place	Summary of Events and Information	Remarks and references to Appendices
BETHUNE	Rested + billeted in the morning all officers were ordered into billets BETHUNE again. No 6. 2nd Bn. took our place. Lt. M. PERN left for the FA and attached R.W. FUSILIERS was wounded & killed when attending wounded between the two lines by Germans.	
12.	A letter of commendation was sent to Lt. Pope by Gen'l JOFFRE for Brillian Standing the by for 15 hrs in May works. Under Capt. O'NEILL 15 horses driven 24 hrs.	
13.	Ambulances provided to take over the School at BEUVRY where we were before. The 1st & 3rd Brigade having marched to CUINCHY trees	Authority ?? 4 CA

Army Form C. 2118.

WAR DIARY
or
INTELLIGENCE SUMMARY

(Erase heading not required.)

Instructions regarding War Diaries and Intelligence Summaries are contained in F. S. Regs., Part II. and the Staff Manual respectively. Title pages will be prepared in manuscript.

Hour, Date, Place	Summary of Events and Information	Remarks and references to Appendices
BETHUNE		
14th	to line other than dead wounded to. The whole of the Bavarian division are at BEURY (they are looking)	
15th	The trains are full to the war area, South of BETHUNE - LEBRANCE Road not KERMELLES as a central point. Lully occupied by the French it is her Commander of our Brigade. We have very long copy? — The 2nd Division being engaged in an attack we tended but by sending our ambulances as before in from wounded at PARIBERT, les trans	Casualties M.G.A.

WAR DIARY
or
INTELLIGENCE SUMMARY
(Erase heading not required.)

Army Form C. 2118.

Instructions regarding War Diaries and Intelligence Summaries are contained in F. S. Regs., Part II. and the Staff Manual respectively. Title pages will be prepared in manuscript.

Hour, Date, Place	Summary of Events and Information	Remarks and references to Appendices
BETHUNE		
May 19.	Four have been wounded from 2nd & 4th Divisions. Lt Sharp comes to No 3 F.A. Still have a good number of wounded men coming through.	
May 20.	Bearer division ones back to GENEVIEVE. In hopes to have us to [ILLEGIBLE MATERNELLE] but it fell through. Later on account of pressure in No. Three New horse Coy & F.A. being moved. Rifle.	
May 22.	We all move out to FOUQUIERES. G. A. Caught horse & bedded on inspect at 2pm. Return to tower of the village. No. 13 have perforce to continue for a while BETHUNE. Later we were busier [C. Gards]	Wellington A C 1

WAR DIARY
or
INTELLIGENCE SUMMARY

(Erase heading not required.)

Army Form C. 2118.

Hour, Date, Place	Summary of Events and Information	Remarks and references to Appendices
FOUQUERES May 25.	We have a fresh threat from aeroplanes to-day. I short time ago today we received word we are again No 1 F.A. from C. Line BEARNE a capt & F. Keeling	
26th	Me arms here (C. ?A)	
27	Capt Cameron got to N.º 7 Co. was kept in Fontinoy dug out & is thence to Lt AM Quellue.	
28	Lecture given upon the Gas which is frequently used here a drill was been in what wear has given the long life wears had to be made. Lt Dick Montier last. Cust Mortar	

Army Form C. 2118.

WAR DIARY
or
INTELLIGENCE SUMMARY
(Erase heading not required.)

Hour, Date, Place	Summary of Events and Information	Remarks and references to Appendices
FOUQUIÈRES May 29th	Nothing to in. Capt. Worthington appointed Acting Q.M. made. Capt. O'Neill put in Charge gun.	
30th	Visit 9th Assur. Front line knife LA BOURRIÈRE to Cuinchy R.A. Enemy work there.	
31st	Remain on at FOUQUIÈRES	Arthayn Lt Col O.C. No 2 C.A.

121/6210

June 1915

1st Division

No 3. Field Ambulance
Vol XI

137/6210

Aus

Army Form C. 2118.

WAR DIARY
or
INTELLIGENCE SUMMARY
(Erase heading not required.)

Instructions regarding War Diaries and Intelligence Summaries are contained in F. S. Regs., Part II. and the Staff Manual respectively. Title pages will be prepared in manuscript.

Hour, Date, Place	Summary of Events and Information	Remarks and references to Appendices
FOUQUIÈRES June 18th	The F.A. is at TREKET at a farm here & 18 horses have been captured. Horses in [illegible] I.S.M. Came out definite system of holding down tracks conveying us to fire [illegible] one day. Returning to rest into a fight as dragoons. [illegible] [illegible] that the toughest respect the brunt of [illegible] with its muzzle the [illegible] stone shells in the [illegible], the [illegible] has at [illegible] to the line.	
June 14th	[illegible] to [illegible] but Capt Gibson & 155 CUINCHY are that we are to leave my HE place from [illegible] [illegible] [illegible] the trenches	Authority [illegible]

Army Form C. 2118.

WAR DIARY
or
INTELLIGENCE SUMMARY
(Erase heading not required.)

Instructions regarding War Diaries and Intelligence Summaries are contained in F. S. Regs., Part II. and the Staff Manual respectively. Title pages will be prepared in manuscript.

Hour, Date, Place	Summary of Events and Information	Remarks and references to Appendices
FOUQUIERES	dismounting station is at No 1 Int. Field [illegible]. The ambulance turns out during [illegible] on a large scale as trains at [illegible] in BÉTHUNE. Evacuation from here to LEAVE been found [illegible] were to be kept open to hold down the sick or injured + any [illegible] provided that the whole [illegible] cases or injury + duty. Return from BÉTHUNE lorry CMT Coys in charge of Medical Company. The officers i/c of the attaches a report of each case + send to march to BÉTHUNE S/Sgt. 2nd Echelon. A chill is to	Ambulance U.C.A.

Army Form C. 2118.

WAR DIARY
or
INTELLIGENCE SUMMARY

(Erase heading not required.)

Instructions regarding War Diaries and Intelligence Summaries are contained in F. S. Regs., Part II. and the Staff Manual respectively. Title pages will be prepared in manuscript.

Hour, Date, Place	Summary of Events and Information	Remarks and references to Appendices
	[handwritten notes, largely illegible]	

WAR DIARY
or
INTELLIGENCE SUMMARY

(Erase heading not required.)

Army Form C. 2118.

Instructions regarding War Diaries and Intelligence Summaries are contained in F. S. Regs., Part II. and the Staff Manual respectively. Title pages will be prepared in manuscript.

Hour, Date, Place	Summary of Events and Information	Remarks and references to Appendices
Forquier June 9th	The battalion was till [illegible] to them for 150 [illegible] of all ranks. 150 [illegible] a refuse was [illegible] given the [illegible] C.O.	
June 10	[illegible] continued to [illegible] this [illegible] 10th [illegible] carried out a number of practical [illegible] in [illegible]. There [illegible] totals are [illegible] [illegible] to C Coy of C Coy was sent to [illegible]. He was sent for a [illegible] hrs.	
June 11th	Capt. [illegible] and his party return to Coy H.Q. from Beaury and Cuinchy in [illegible]. C./No1 F.A. Grant	Au [illegible] W.C.A

1247 W 3299 200,000 (E) 8/14 J.B.C. & A. Forms/C. 2118/11.

WAR DIARY
or
INTELLIGENCE SUMMARY

Army Form C. 2118.

(*Erase heading not required.*)

Instructions regarding War Diaries and Intelligence Summaries are contained in F. S. Regs., Part II. and the Staff Manual respectively. Title pages will be prepared in manuscript.

Hour, Date, Place	Summary of Events and Information	Remarks and references to Appendices
FOUQUIÈRES. June 27th	Awful wet Tuesday through the had been disturbed by Captain Witherla. A child with severe burns of head also been here	
June 28th	Move at 1.45 to AUCHEL where the men leave in a field and a hospital is opened at the HOTEL de VILLE. Return via MARLES les MINES to FOUQUIÈRES. The night of June 28/29 is spent at CHATEAU de CHARMEAUX, GOSNAY.	
June 29	Arrive at FOUQUIÈRES where the cable was. It grows again from Next F.A.	Ambulance War O.E.N.D.& F.A.
June 30	The hospital is again open for V couplin P. Pillotti	

Army Form C. 2118.

WAR DIARY
or
INTELLIGENCE SUMMARY

(Erase heading not required.)

Instructions regarding War Diaries and Intelligence Summaries are contained in F. S. Regs., Part II. and the Staff Manual respectively. Title pages will be prepared in manuscript.

Hour, Date, Place	Summary of Events and Information	Remarks and references to Appendices
FOUQUEREUIL		
June 14.	[illegible handwritten entry]	
June 15th	[illegible handwritten entry]	
June 17th	[illegible handwritten entry]	
June 18th	[illegible handwritten entry]	
June 19th	[illegible handwritten entry]	
June 20	[illegible handwritten entry]	

To Gen Dir 24/8/15

18/6210

12/6210

1st Division

No 3 Field Ambulance

July 1915

Army Form C. 2118.

WAR DIARY
or
INTELLIGENCE SUMMARY

(Erase heading not required.)

Instructions regarding War Diaries and Intelligence Summaries are contained in F. S. Regs., Part II. and the Staff Manual respectively. Title pages will be prepared in manuscript.

Hour, Date, Place	Summary of Events and Information	Remarks and references to Appendices
FOUQUIÈRES July 1st. 1915.	All the field ambulances here at the present time are all taking in the sick of the division and all convalescents.	
2.	No 2 F.A. having today sent in 30 patients for treatment	
4th	There was shelling at VERQUIN there are 3 women and two civilians came here for treatment. Key one case serious —	
5th	Today Captain Mulgrew made an inspection of the lines & houses & found them satisfactory.	
10.0	Rode with Colonel ...... on the VERMELLES and CAMBRIN areas. I visited the area with Captain Workington today & made arrangements for huts been divided to take our trenches. The dressing station is to be at SAILLY LEBOURSE will clearing posts under a M.O. both at CAMBRIN and VERMELLES.	

WAR DIARY or INTELLIGENCE SUMMARY

Army Form C. 2118.

(Erase heading not required.)

Instructions regarding War Diaries and Intelligence Summaries are contained in F. S. Regs., Part II. and the Staff Manual respectively. Title pages will be prepared in manuscript.

Hour, Date, Place	Summary of Events and Information	Remarks and references to Appendices
July 11th	In front of this again, a detachment is to be posted at Pierce Farm located on Sugg's and Bart's where parties can be taken out from the reserved shelter trenches. Owing to the lack of communication trenches the horse-lines of the Battalion cannot be used by day, and so the ahead head cloaking huts of canvas poles, in which a head cloaking huts of canvas poles, in which a line can be carried on a billing position are being provided, and it is proposed to have the 1st Inny. Capt. Smith (Engrs) is i/c of arrangts. Captain Anderson (?) has Coln i/c charge of same on July 13.	
July 12th	As there is no room for horse-lines close to Cours d'Chatteau VERNEILLES, permission was granted for (a) teams to return the Echelon (?) to Cours. [three lines illegible]	

1247 W 3299 200,000 (E) 8/14 J.B.C. & A. Forms/C. 2118/11.

WAR DIARY
or
INTELLIGENCE SUMMARY

(Erase heading not required.)

Army Form C. 2118.

Hour, Date, Place	Summary of Events and Information	Remarks and references to Appendices
July 15	Car broken. Next at G. SAILLY LE BOURSE billets, and draft at Cuiltin. Consult I. and C. attached to us (Gunforming) for duty etc. Came across went on duty leave Sunday 12 noon	Arthur O'Neill
July 13th	Took over things from Lt. Col. Hooper, DAD when we leave yesterday. Received the following instructions from A.D.M.S. 9th Div. I. To instruct the O.C. Bear. Division (Capt. Worthington (RMS)) at SAILLY LABOURSE to evacuate all their casualties wounded & sick via, as to 2 F.A. was running from BETHUNE to ANNEZIN. II. To instruct Adv. Div. Surgeon that they are responsible for the collection if casualties too among the Indian Cavalry who are nothing in the area ANNEQUIN - NOYELLES.	P. M. O'Neill Capt. R.A.M.C.

Army Form C. 2118.

WAR DIARY
or
INTELLIGENCE SUMMARY
(Erase heading not required.)

Instructions regarding War Diaries and Intelligence Summaries are contained in F. S. Regs., Part II. and the Staff Manual respectively. Title pages will be prepared in manuscript.

Hour, Date, Place	Summary of Events and Information	Remarks and references to Appendices
July 21st	Under instructions from A.D.M.S. 1st Div. detailed Lieut. O. Walsh. R.A.M.C. to relieve Capt. Dale R.A.M.C. M.O. w/c 2nd Welsh Regt. who was proceeding on leave.	
July 22nd	A party of 4 officers & 20 men from 15th F.A. 1st Div. joined for instruction. Three officers & 16 men (Beaver) sent to SAILLY LABOURSE for duty with Beaver Div. five officers & 4 men retained for duty at H.Q.	
July 23rd	The Beaver Division reference Hq from SAILLY LABOURSE, CAMBRIN + VERMELLES to relieved by the Beaver Division of No. 1 F.A.	
July 25th	Capt Matthews on No. 18 0.1 three men proceeded on leave.	E. M. O'Neill Capt. R.A.M.C.

WAR DIARY
or
INTELLIGENCE SUMMARY

(Erase heading not required.)

Army Form C. 2118.

Hour, Date, Place	Summary of Events and Information	Remarks and references to Appendices
Aug 26th	Reserve Office of F.A. on 1st leave to England	
" 27th	Col had notice that F.A. has been [?] to return to	
" 28th	Capt Antrim left to R.F.A. to return [?] Anxiously [?] for news. Lt Grant [?] down [?] to duty for S.A. Antrim on 14 [August] W.R.	
29th	The F.A. held Sports C[?] [?] [?] Whistles.	
30th	Party of 500 from Regiment at LA BUISSIÈRE. The order to [?] small regiment to [?] to have remained between [?] relief to [?]	
31st	[?] Pann from the C[?] [?] & [?] (adjy) duty until to return & Capt [?].	Anthony [?] f. ca.

www.ingramcontent.com/pod-product-compliance
Lightning Source LLC
Chambersburg PA
CBHW081439160426

43193CB00013B/2325